Terminal Diagnosis

Terminal Diagnosis

Poems by

Bill Glose

Cover design by Shay Culligan
Cover image by Hemanth Nirujogi on Unsplash
Author photo by Bill Glose

ISBN: 979-8-90146-899-9
Library of Congress Control Number: 2026937981

Kelsay Books
502 South 1040 East, A-119
American Fork, Utah 84003
Kelsaybooks.com

For Dawn West,
for her bravery and steadfast lust for life
in the face of devastating news.

Acknowledgments

I am grateful to the following publications where these poems first appeared, sometimes in slightly different form:

Amsterdam Quarterly: "I Never Know When It's Going to Rain"
Artemis Journal: "Hurricane" (originally published as "Wind Shear")
Blue Collar Review: "Salpingo-oophorectomy"
Blueline: "Seven Deer," "Hoarfrost" (originally published as "Sunday Frost")
Borderlands: Texas Poetry Review: "Breathings of the Moon"
The Broadkill Review: "Making Plans"
California Quarterly: "Escape Hatch"
Capable: "Road Therapy"
Comstock Review: "Making Love to the Terminally Ill," "Scrub of a Once-Soft Spot"
DASH Literary Journal: "Revising Her Will"
Front Range Review: "PET Scan"
Golden Laureates: "Harbinger"
The Heartland Review: "Singer"
Literary Accents: "Giving Up"
The Midwest Quarterly: "Inner Workings," "Waiting" (originally published as "Waiting for Something to Happen")
Mud Season Review: "Road Trip to Duke"
The Northern Virginia Review: "Alchemy," "At the Homeopathic Clinic"; *Plainsongs:* "Necessary Lies"
Poetry Virginia: "Things Left Unsaid"
Potomac Review: "Grocery Shopping"
Quiet Diamonds: "Stardust"

Rattle: "Sasquatch," "Second Opinion"
Schuylkill Valley Journal: "First Face"
SLANT Poetry Journal: "Dictionary of the Dying"
South 85 Journal: "How Fast It Grows"
Still You: Poems of Illness & Healing: "Ephemera"
Streetlight Magazine: "Time Traveling"
Tar River Poetry: "A Galaxy of Astronauts"
THEMA: "Telling the Judge"

Contents

I.
BEFORE

Photo Op

Dawn says a purple sky means
the heart of someone you know
has been bruised. In a grassy sward
where tourists cluster around
placards in reverence, waning sun
strikes Revolutionary cannons,
shadows thrown long at my feet.
Instead of aiming my camera
at iron barrels or the zig-zag,
split-rail fence forming
a skirmish line beside
the gravel parking lot,
I capture Dawn as she runs,
                    laughing,

towing her new, red kite,
bobbling on a string
like bumper-tied cans
behind a couple "Just Married."
Shaped like a biplane with
a fluttering tail, the kite
never rises more than ten feet,
corkscrewing in her wake
as she races back and forth,
chasing fog-wreathed memories
of how easy it had been
in pastures of our youth,
every remembered whim
capturing air to climb
into clouds, trying like hell
to carry us along.

Divine

Unwitnessed moments need no trumpet
for grace—the back-bent seeding

of a garden, scrubbing of a kitchen sink,
genuflected praying for a loved one.

I didn't know Dawn when she built
the bridge in the gully behind her house,

but when I gaze now upon its tired arch
spanning the streambed, planks

gone spongy and soft, railings twined
with brambled threads of honeysuckle,

I can see her as if I did, our shared winters
giving way to the memory of spring.

There she is, long braid down her back,
hammer in hand, pausing to survey the woods

and see how many plants she can name.

How We Met

New Year’s Eve,
a mutual friend’s house
overlooking water,

its blue glass a bed for stars
and the quarter of moon
not yet swallowed.

The petulant calendar
clung to its last page
and all the year’s sins,

forestalling
midnight’s arrival.
Inside, amid

ubiquitous glissandos
of laughter, I roved
from one flock

of sequined gowns
to the next,
clasping a plate

of canapes
and crackers
like a prop.

Upstairs,
behind a barking door,
I found you

with the host's two collies,
party dress hiked to thighs
as you squatted to scratch

behind their ears. My spine
felt the twining of our DNA
before we'd even said hello,

before our night-long
conversation spooled
into each other's helix,

before I raced to water's edge
to help shoot fireworks,
their explosions bathing you

at the top of a hill,
your upturned face
glimmering.

Promise

Once a week, Dawn visits Carol,
a friend tethered to oxygen tanks
by clear plastic tubes that hook
over ears to a nasal cannula.

They'd spent years together
in the jails, Dawn, a deputy
who manhandled convicts
twice her size, Carol,

a nurse who took no shit
from those she treated,
bedside manner hard
as tempered steel.

I went along once
to Carol's home, now a cell,
front door dead-bolted,
air thick as gauze,

every shade shut
against sun and splashes
of purple from crepe myrtles
in a neighbor's yard.

Between rhythmic spurts
of air from a silver tank,
Carol rasped desire
for another cigarette.

On the drive home,
windows gulped
the breath of spring
as we raced back

to our blessed lives,
scrolling landscape of green
and blue like a painting
with no vanishing point.

If I ever get like that,
Dawn said, *promise me*
you'll pull the plug.
God help me, I said I would.

Seven Deer

In the near-still murk of dusk,
slow as the beat of a sleeping heart,

a family of deer graze amid hickory
and pines, brown on brown, rustle

of dead leaves the only hint of passage.
My deer, Dawn says, elbows propped

on the railing of her back deck, hair
freed from its bun, a waterfall of gold.

Funny what things we claim possession—
countries and continents, a specific hour

of the day, luck, good and bad.
Why not these animals, this moment?

The buck turns his eight-point rack
to stare back at us as two fawns

with fading spots lap at a salt lick,
and just as Dawn smiles at me,

a winking firefly flits between us,
its trail glowing like a spark of magic.

Harbinger

On the welcome mat
outside Dawn’s back door,

her cat has been leaving gifts—
Carolina wrens with broken necks,

moles with velvet fur
and star-shaped noses,

now limp as a failed notion—
and she wonders what it means.

Only knowledge I can offer is
my belief in science and formulas,

probabilities and statistics,
tensile strengths of materials.

I appreciate the beauty of a bell curve
and likelihood of multiple outcomes,

facts as unhelpful as they are
unwanted. So, I stay silent

and hold the ladder in Dawn’s foyer
as she climbs its rubberized steps

to water plants on the ledge, their vines
trailing down the faux brick façade,

my hands on her calves as I look up,
hoping she won’t fall.

Making Plans

In bed this morning, she clung
to Caribbean dreams of topaz water
and white sand, calypso music
and fruity drinks with umbrellas,
avoiding her annual physical.

All week she's eyed the calendar's
red circle like a dog unwilling
to step outside, front legs stiff, claws
dug into shag. *If I never go,* she argues,
he can't find something wrong.

Pushing her out the door, I promise
the doctor will find nothing amiss
and that we'll meet afterwards
in the park, a languorous stroll
beneath a plump sun lolling
in endless sky.

No reason to think otherwise.
No reason not to pack a lunch.

II.
DURING

Chrysalis

On her x-ray,
a dot of pure white
nestles between
curling slats of ribs,

burrowing into a lung.
Hung in a gallery,
this brilliant contrast
could be high art,

one body shimmering
within shadows
of another,
cocooned in gray

like a chrysalis,
a burgeoning pupa
waiting to erupt
into something wild.

Waiting

There is no terror in the bang, only in anticipation of it.
—Alfred Hitchcock

Each lost day is tiny, a single shard
in scatterings of broken glass.

Given time, erosion can nullify mountains,
once-strong shoulders slumping into silt.

We like to think we're prepared
for calamity, but no one knows when

or where a meteor will strike.
Only comets warn us with their tails,

icy plumes erupting from a sun
whose gravity they can't escape.

When Hale-Bopp streaked past Earth,
some spread checkered blankets

on grassy knolls to picnic;
others committed suicide.

One moonless night, trekking
past farms with my girlfriend—

who now either *has* a tumor
or *does not*—

past barns with flaking, red paint
and silos with rust-threaded seams,

I asked her to lie in the road.
Dawn didn't trust me

until I dropped down myself,
back pressed to crown of cool tar,

upturned face collecting stars, each point
of light travelling billions of miles

to grace this moment.
As we lay wordlessly,

a satellite transected the sky,
its red eye winking in time

with the beat
of my astonished heart.

Second Opinion

Woodpeckers hammer bark in search
of insects or sap; yellow-sleeved arms
of forsythia wave hello; a girl in pink shorts
and pigtails chalks her driveway,
curious tongue peeking from the corner
of her mouth—each wonder noticed
and discussed on the long drive
to the second doctor's office.

We've dreamed this white-smocked sage
will decry the first, sifting scans and charts,
shaking an error free from silt. He'll point to it
like I am doing now to the hummingbird
hovering impossibly at a feeder,
lapping from a silver spout of nectar.

Not that we'll remember it later,
slouching up front steps, crossing
the living room and falling on the couch,
dogs with dire eyes lying beside us,
the smell of something sour in the air,
and me, suddenly quiet, weight
of every word like rocks on my tongue.

Necessary Lies

This won't hurt a bit, says the doctor,
foot-long needle filling his fist,
faith in anesthesia absolute
from his side of the table.

Dawn lies face-down
in an open-backed smock,
slats of her ribs stark
as a white picket fence.

Beneath her armpit,
he thrusts with all his weight
like a brute
breaking down a door,

and as her hand
vises mine, I wonder
how much of life's passage
is greased by lies.

When my fifth-grade class
cut apart frogs, pinned
skin to trays, plucked out
hearts and other organs,

our teacher promised
that the dead
would not reanimate
and haunt our dreams.

It takes this moment
beside my girlfriend
laid out on butcher paper
like a landed fish

for me to understand
these lies are spoken
to soften
our own pillows.

And so I pat her
trembling hand,
whisper in her ear
how I'm sure

the biopsy will be negative,
how life will go on
as it always had,
how outside the window

a gray-cheeked thrush
is whistling just for her.

Hoarfrost

Like creeping age, it sidles up
while backs are turned,

whispers hard truths
to all that is soft and warm.

Into a bed of grass it settles
with its bucket of white,

patient as a new moon
shrouded by night's ink.

Every mundane tuft
varnished until each blade

                    becomes infinite,
flattened scruffs

rising into shimmering
coats of armor as if

to challenge the coming sun.
Soon enough, a choir

will crunch across their
brittle backs, file into pews,

sing, *This, too, shall pass.*
For now, the only hymn

is silence, the glittering
silver of its tongue.

PET Scan

A positron emission tomography (PET) scan is an imaging test that helps reveal how your tissues and organs are functioning. A PET scan uses a radioactive drug (tracer) to show this activity.
—MAYO Clinic website

Blue-smocked technicians fiddle
with controls on the other side

of a double layer of safety glass.
They could be NASA engineers

and she a rocket set to launch
through this tube into space,

searching for planets that orbit stars
at just the right distance for liquid water—

a *Goldilocks* zone, not too close,
not too far away. Possibilities swim

through her harness-locked head
while dragging inhalations undulate

like an ocean lapping
the inner shore of her chest.

Earlier, rubber-gloved hands
injected a radioactive tracer

that coursed up her arm
like ice water after a spring thaw.

A nurse promised the procedure
was safe before warning her

to stay away from pregnant women
and children the next six hours.

Unlike an MRI's jackhammering,
this tube hums like a fridge,

something ears don't register
until the motor shudders off.

The chill long gone, she's as warm
as when she was a little girl

lying in a field of cornflowers,
staring at the sky's vast blue,

imagining the atmosphere
as a giant raindrop

and she a creature caught within,
underwater, yet still able to breathe.

Telling the Judge

News of her illness staggers the judge,
one hand tearing his gray hair,
black robe tossed over his chair's
oak back. He doesn't cry, this wiry man
who executes 100 pushups every day.
But he hugs Dawn hard, crushing her
against his striped tie and the gold bar
holding it to his shirt.

I only witnessed Dawn in court once
as she performed bailiff duties,
blond bun tight on her head, stern jab
of a finger in the face of anyone
talking out of turn. She marched
manacled prisoners from a side door
to face the judge, like a second father,
someone she could not *not tell.*

Louise, too,
the clerk who rolled her eyes
at defendants' weak excuses
and celebrated ends of long days
with salt-rimmed margaritas.
She must tell them, but no one else.

Can't let them see you weak,
a lesson from the judge, he who
once said he wouldn't use an umbrella
even if it was raining hammers.

Imagine

Imagine Tyrannosaurus Rex
at the height of his reign,

head the size of a Volkswagen,
bone-crushing jaws lined with spikes,

fear as foreign a concept as comets
falling from sky. Imagine

the moment it all changed,
flash of light tearing the world apart,

turning it to ash. The sun
blotted out, air choked with dust.

Can you feel the clog of particles
in your lungs, in your

air-conditioned home? If you
close your eyes, can you feel

the walls ablaze, an invisible hand
squeezing your chest?

That's all it takes—*a blink*—
for life to change,

for blue skies
to split with fire,

for kindling of your ribs
to spark and burn.

Sasquatch

Dawn and I once spent a night in a Bigfoot-hunter's cabin
on the border between Virginia and her un-seceded sister.
Our host led us into woods where camouflaged,

motion-sensor cameras were strapped to trees.
We wore thermal-vision headsets as he stomped
in the distance, his red form glowing amid the green.

In the cabin, he showed off ultrasonic airborne probes,
sheaves of data, and plaster molds of gigantic feet.
Twenty years earlier, he'd seen the creature

and has been chasing ever since. On cold nights
after another fruitless hunt, surely his logical mind
must wonder if that glimpse had been a trickster's hoax

and the past two decades a waste of time.
You've got to have faith, he crowed
from that perch no argument can knock down.

And what is there to say when a fawn proclaims
it's not a deer but a leopard? *Just look at my spots.*
I'm a hawk, says the robin. *I'm a constellation,* the bear.

I'm alive, say the dead in caskets' pillowed linings.
Once, at a Catholic wedding in a cavernous, church,
Dawn was mesmerized by stained-glass windows, hymnals

with gilt-limned pages, tapestries that hung for miles.
But all I saw were the pews' hard backs, tithing envelopes,
Jesus on the cross, weeping eyes imploring me to run.

Knowing how far I'd fallen, Dawn rejoiced
when I remembered the proper words, the call
and response of praise, its rhythm worn into knees.

What is *faith* but knowing something to be true
when evidence tells you it is not? I've always turned
to science for illumination; Dawn turns her face

to the sky. It's why, in our cabin room,
when I picked apart the Bigfoot myth,
Dawn shook me and said, *Just enjoy the moment.*

Next morning, as the hunter turned pages
of a photo album, one wooded spot after another
where sightings had supposedly occurred,

Dawn stood sockless beside white plaster molds
of footprints large enough to swallow the moon,
her red-toenailed feet like a toddler's in comparison.

The dog in my throat wanted to growl,
but I yanked its leash. Sometimes an answer
only comes when you don't know the question.

Visitation

—After the painting *The Annunciation* by Rembrandt

And what of the angel obfuscating with prophecy,
nimbused promises conforming to desire,

bathed with light from a mistaken star?
Do you need a heart to have a heart?

A billion networked nerves to feel pain?
Floating at the foot of the lovelorn,

the lost, the desperate, awash in prayers,
the angel has heard it all before,

knows what tapestry
their fraying threads will weave.

Revising Her Will

Shuffling through the house, she assesses
artwork and baubles, furniture and jewelry.

Hates imagining these rooms dispossessed,
contents stickered at a yard sale or dumped

in trash. How many times has she re-gifted
something unwanted or offered up a white lie

brimming with false sincerity? If she could,
she'd bequeath the gold of her hair

to someone in need, her sense of whimsy
to a neighbor who plods home each evening

with his neck bent to driveway,
eyes heavy as lead. She asks me

to take her dogs, her niece the house,
and the sky to take back the stars

that circle her head when she laughs
so hard she almost passes out.

Inner Workings

In the factory, bleary-eyed nights bled
beneath ceaseless candescence, stacking arms
hammered, and razor-edged slitters
dissected an inked web spun
from two-ton rolls of paper.

All it took was   one   careless   moment
for the machine next to mine to snag its operator
and yank her arm into its hydraulic press.

All wounds should be like that—slashed open
          with crimson painting a clotted stain
                    across dust-flecked steel
of machinery brought suddenly to a halt.
They should howl into night's cavern
                    beneath sudden, shocked silence.
                              And in the wide-eyed hush,
          in the gathered-round crowd
of shuffling, steel-toed boots,
                    in the alert light's strobing flash,

everyone
                    should take
                              a moment

to ponder how fragile a body truly is,
how precious this mortal gift,
the inner workings sheathed in skin.

Road Trip to Duke

Not once on the long trip down
do we mention our motive,

the manila-enveloped passenger in back,
the magnetically-resonanced images

and sheaf of medical assessments.
We play games instead, racing

through alphabets, cataloguing
state slogans, slug-bugging shoulders.

A Virginia sign proclaims
This county invented Brunswick Stew,

and you tell me you once visited a Ruritan
where gallons of stew simmered

in a five-foot vat, stirred with an oar
big enough to paddle a boat.

At Duke University, we stroll
through campus, all those

Gothic spires and crenellations,
grand arches fit for a parade.

Last stop is the Medical Center,
avoided until the weight we're dragging

sticks in its furrow,
ploughshare snapped on stone.

The trip home is quiet,
you, reclining, pretending to doze,

me, staring at the double-yellow line,
wondering how anything

can be so straight and simple.
We stop for dinner

in Brunswick County,
but no restaurants have stew

on the menu, and all the stores
on Main Street are boarded up.

The Cry of Laughter

How could I not fall smiling
into the chorus of shrieking giggles,
girls and boys in glowing sneakers

racing their raucous laughter in circles,
a whirlwind pulling me to its core,
stripping away years until

memory of my youth runs alongside.
The breeze is light, the grass green,
and everywhere the scent of spring.

The leaden ache I've been dragging
forgotten for a moment, lying
on the ground like a sun-dazed dog

freed from its leash, panting
in a pool of shade.
Soon enough it starts to growl,

and gravity reasserts itself,
heart heavy with guilt
for having felt such glee

when my love is at home,
                    sick in bed.

The children continue playing, heedless
of the yellow school bus rumbling their way
and where it will one day take them.

Ephemera

Half-drunk mugs on the coffee table
spread rings like a farmer sowing seed.

Laundry gathers in hampers, dishes in the sink.
The vacuum stands in the corner like a girl

in a hand-me-down dress hoping someone
will ask her to dance. Life's fractions sliced so thin

that light streams through without blinking,
wedges of pie needing companions to make a whole.

Wrapped in an aqua Snuggie, Dawn zones out
as television's talking heads recount the day's woes—

rapes and murders, corporate pillaging, bombs
blown up in crowds—background buzz blotting out

any need for conscious thought. Anchors stare
at the screen, peering into our living room,

capped smiles swallowed by dour expressions
as if noticing the manila envelope stamped

"Biopsy Results," the sheath weighed down
with a bulging purse as if it might blow away.

Tug of War

As I pull a knotted rope-toy,
Dawn's gray-muzzled Rottweiler
yanks the other end rhythmically,
        her head jerking down,
loosening,
        then down again,
almost ripping my arm from socket.
Most afternoons she's itinerant,
migrating across carpet
from one square of light
to another, curling snout-to-tail
in the warm oven of lost hours.
But today, her age has shipped off
on some long-forgotten schooner,
its hold freighted with her arthritis
and all my worries, howling fears
that usually demand attention.
So I let go of the rope
                and everything else,
reveling in the dog's romping joy
as she races round the coffee table
then back, dropping her spoils
at my feet, eyes fixed on my hand
like a child watching her mother
layer icing on a cake, knowing
how she'll get to lick the spoon
after the last dollop is smeared.

Dog Room

A space marked on blueprints
as an office or study tucked into
the hallway's elbow, now repurposed
as a home within a home. On the far wall
is a bed with legs made from two-by-fours
and topped with a beanbag mattress
where two Rottweilers sleep
like womb-twined twins.

Blue sky pours through windowpanes
smeared with nose prints, splashing
across carpet worn smooth
as grass in a batter's circle.
Scattered about are knotted ropes,
gnawed hooves, and bit-off chunks
of rubber toys. All that keeps the dogs
from racing through the house
is half a homemade Dutch door,
one foot high, easy enough to jump,
except they've been trained not to.

Most times it's unlatched, and they roam
where they please. But on days
filled with black clouds, they huddle
under the bed, barely enough space
to squeeze beneath its planks,
close comfort of this one spot
a refuge from the world's thunder.

Time Traveling

Driving switchbacks on Shenandoah's spine,
dipping into valleys and screaming up again,

we scorch speed warnings from yellow diamonds
as the dashboard Garmin's destination time

spins backwards. We're regaining invisible minutes
that would have languished on a longer voyage,

one that slowed to marvel at purple splashes
of ironweed and white tassels of sweetspire

or braked to heed warnings of falling rocks.
The cerulean sky has tumbled other sarsens

in our path, and instead of ringing them
in monuments, we have taken to the road,

racing time itself, arms stretched out windows,
splayed fingers clawing the howling wind.

Measurements

A human brain is the size of an oblong volleyball.
Your stomach, the size of a grapefruit, can balloon

to a watermelon when stuffed. Lungs, delicate
as butterfly wings, light as papier-mâché,

span rib cages from collarbone to gut.
Where bronchioles narrow to clustered alveoli,

red blood cells plump with oxygen and race off
to nourish our bodies. In the pleural sac surrounding

Dawn's right lung sits a two-centimeter spot, smaller
than a walnut, small enough to roll in my hand

like a marble. So little for something that can
swallow a universe. An average human heart,

the size and shape of a fist, pumps 1.2 gallons of blood
through 100,000 miles of vessels. Next time

you're in the grocery store, pick up a jug of milk,
imagine it scarlet, think, *This is all I am.*

Pour its contents over gleaming tiles, let it slop
beneath shelves stocked with brightly painted boxes

whose slogans insinuate importance in our lives.
Regard the spill and think, *This is all I'll ever be.*

Salpingo-oophorectomy

Like muck from a pumpkin, both ovaries
and fallopian tubes scooped out
when the first cancer invaded. The surgeon,
he of the better-safe-than-sorry school,
removed *all* lymph nodes from her groin.
Afterwards, lymphedema transformed skin
into a substance like Memory Foam.
"Mummy School" taught her to wrap legs
in yards of Ace bandage, to massage
pooling liquid back toward missing nodes,
to struggle into a compression garment
every morning so skin wouldn't plump
to elephantine proportions. Then bursting.
The thick garment, rubbery as a diving suit,
squeezes every inch from waist to toes.
No more dresses. No more swimming.
No more basking in sun. And now,
years later, one more thing to surrender—
radiation and chemotherapy. Her system
can endure no more poison, even to attack
a new plague. Everything is connected,
a lesson learned in kindergarten.
Knee bone to thigh bone. Thigh bone to hip.
Dominoes can stand on end forever.
Unless one totters. Then all fall down.

Breathings of the Moon

At every rising and every setting of the moon
the sea violently covers the coast far and wide . . .
unwittingly drawn up by some breathings of the moon.
—Saint Bede in *Opera de Temporibus* (703 AD)

Caught in a glass tube,
a ball floats on a cushion of air
between two ink lines

as Dawn blows in a mouthpiece.
Just one of the pulmonary clinic's toys,
each apparatus testing volume

and longevity, the functioning
of bronchioles and alveoli, the delivery
of each air sac's clustered promises.

Here, *inspiration* and *expiration*
mean something other
than creativity and loss.

A scan of Dawn's lungs develops
in the other room, slow as a Polaroid,
and the technician says not to worry.

Young and not yet beaten down,
he tells Dawn her capacity is that
of a twenty-year-old as her pale features

turn burgundy. Ignorant of gravity,
early man once compared the way
our moon influenced oceans

with the rise and fall of a breathing body,
cresting surf bringing life to shore
before a vanishing tide stole it all back.

She asks why

and I answer without answering,
the old psychologist's trick,
feeding one question with another.
Why does anything happen at all?

A vagary meant to sidetrack
conversation toward metaphysics,
multitudinous miracles of life,
all its infinite wonders and tragedies.

Long ago, as children, we believed
everything we were told,
our niggling and never-ending
curiosity sparking through dry tinder.

But long ago was long ago, and Dawn
no longer believes monsters hide
in her closet or under her bed.
They lurk, instead, on X-rays,

shadows where none should be,
black flags unfurling over a sea of bones.
Why me and not them? she asks,
pointing at the television,

mugshots of home-invaders
snarling on the screen,
remorseless after beating
a geriatric couple to death.

I could mention the randomness of existence,
the gorgeous tapestry arising from
a billion interwoven happenstances.
But experience has shown where that

thread leads—toward the unfairness
of life on Earth, the indifference
with which God drops his hammer
on saved and sinner alike.

How about a walk? I say.
We can bring the dogs.
I call over the two Rottweilers
and they lean against our legs,

heads resting in laps, patient
as our hands scrub their fur
in search of answers, willing
to stand there for as long as it takes.

Making Love to the Terminally Ill

Like an oft-whipped dog
still longing to please,

I slink into bed,
ardor twined with dread.

But I am just a man
and she the woman

who stirs my blood.
Insistence dire

as a murder of crows,
she guides me to her center,

that silken throat
that swallows inhibition

and leaves it gasping.
So easy to believe

promises of rapture,
urgency of moans,

squeeze of thighs and rake
of nails. When worry

presses between our bodies
with its wedge of memory—

all those times before we've tried
and halted, passion interrupted

by gasps for breath and bouts of crying—
my eyelids squeeze so tightly

that stars blind with brilliance,
mouth full of her flesh,

teeth biting hard enough to score
without breaking the surface.

Afterwards, we savor
sweet stillness, her spine

curled against my chest,
my hand cupping her breast,

palm filled with every torn thing
that lies beneath.

Escape Hatch

Perched in the cup of a wingback chair,
feet tucked beneath her like a rabbit
ready to spring, Dawn cranes her neck

toward the window and pattering rain
that scrubs away yellow pollen. Soon,
the dripping drumbeats will give way

to croaking frogs and songs of birds
seeking mates. Hooded eyes fixed
on the waterlogged scene, Dawn says,

You didn't sign up for this, rueful,
like someone trying on a dress
she can't afford before slipping it off

to step back into jeans. Her voice
trembles when she offers me the out.
As if I were a pilot and she the jet

whose single engine failed. As if I'd eject
and follow billowing silk into blue sky
before searching for someplace soft to land.

Stages of Grief

How do these geese know when to fly to the sun?
Who tells them the seasons? How do we, humans,
know when it is time to move on?
—Dr. Elisabeth Kübler-Ross from *The Wheel of Life*

I. Denial

When the oncologist suggests
preparing for the end,
Dawn buys a motorcycle.

No longer afraid
of consequences,
of what might happen

if she crashes.
Driving hard
as if racing

from truth.
You can deny
gravity is real

until you step
off a ledge
and fall.

II. Anger

Shopping for housewares
at Walmart, standing
in the aisle

of five-year bulbs,
fists clenched,
chest thrust

like the figurehead
on a schooner's prow.
No, she yells,

jolting nearby shoppers,
I won't buy a damn bulb
that outlives me!

III. Bargaining

A rosary in the glass dish
atop her vanity. Sculptures
of winged cherubs

in the garden. Horseshoes
and pineapples for good luck.
Parades of elephants

throughout her house,
each trunk raised. African
“spirit masks” on the wall.

A dog-eared book
at her bedside—
The Secrets

of Shambhala:
In Search of
the Eleventh Insight.

Depending on her mood,
the three-headed statue
of Trimurti is turned to show

Brahma the creator,
Vishnu the preserver,
or Shiva the destroyer.

IV. Depression

And when her face wears
the thousand-yard stare
of soldiers too long at war,

I sit beside her
on the couch,
hand-in-hand,

shared silence
saying more
than words.

V. Acceptance

Not all geese fly south.
Some stay
yearlong

at the lake I circle
each morning.
A doddering gander

and his mate feed on
tossed heels of bread
and other forms of grace,

hunkering in a patch
of umbrella sedge,
shaded by all

they've ever known,
sensing the coming winter
but refusing to budge.

How Fast It Grows

In a photo album's vinyl sleeves,
Virginia's Blue Ridge carves
slump-shouldered outlines
against a cerulean sky.

Redbuds sprout from cracks
between stone, and a boulder
worn down by rivulets
wears the face of a wizened man.

On the last pages, kudzu spirals up
train trestles and blackjack oaks,
strangling, smothering,
swallowing mountainsides whole.

Amazing, Dawn had said,
how fast it grows, snapping pictures,
seeing beauty in green blankets,
not choking death that lay beneath.

Even when kudzu's vines are shorn,
its pods can lay dormant underground,
rising up years later to re-infest.

Like cancer, is what we both think now
but dare not say, as she closes the book,
stows it in the bottom drawer of her dresser.

Scrub of a Once-Soft Spot

It was just a silly game
we played
when regrets

were dogs
curled on
someone else's floor.

In tangled sheets,
in moments
of spent breath,

as her fingers stroked
furrows through hairs
on my sweaty chest,

she'd ask,
Would you still love me
if I lost a leg?

If fire
charred my skin?
If I was paralyzed

and had to feed
from a tube?
Would you love me then?

Each time
I'd answer *Yes,*
never imagining

dark angels
bunching wings
into fists

to knock upon our door.
She never asked
if I would love her

if cancer sprouted
in her lung,
but on nights like this,

I wish she would
so I could answer
Yes

one more time,
pulling her body
against mine

beneath crisp sheets
unwrinkled
for weeks.

Reading Hieroglyphs

Without a Rosetta Stone, shifting sand
buries the dog-faced Anubis before
I can translate my dying girlfriend's moods.

Reading hieroglyphs takes patience.
Rebus principle of phonograms is foreign
to Western tongues—pictographs

representing sounds, not objects themselves.
The square symbol for house combines with
an oval mouth to form the word *leave.*

Her mouth says *leave.* And though I stand
my ground, I excavate with subtle strokes,
whisking so quietly it's as if I'm not even there.

First Face

Dawn never knows me as coward,
                    never witnesses the worry
threading my fiber
          on mornings I wake before her,
thankful the god of internal clocks
          grants me time
to hide my *first* face,
          time to form the mask
that proclaims, *I believe in miracles.*

Lying on her side, golden hair
          a fan on flowered sheets,
no sign of cancer in pink flush,
          no sense of dismay on her brow.
Fear waits for eyelids to open,
          interior accountants
                    assessing debits,
balancing ledgers.

No one but me
          sees those trembling moments
                    as dreams dissipate into mist,
          the first face she sloughs off
each morning,
          her features hardening
for the day ahead.

Grocery Shopping

Across Food Lion's gleaming floors,
she steers the prow of her steel-caged cart
away from aisles she knows by rote

toward products once deemed too rich, too fat.
Everything falls into the cart's mesh mouth—
deviled cakes sealed in cling wrap,

tubs of caramel corn, Nestle Combo-Packs
of ice-cream drumsticks poured into
Butterfinger-dipped cones. In the cool clutch

of air-conditioning, anonymity abounds,
each patron intent on their own hoard.
No one's pity plucks apart her skin

as if concern alone could cure the tumor
deep within. No one pries with paring knives,
blind to the way responses spool from her

like flensed fat off a still-warm corpse.
No one weighs her down with tales
of those who beat the odds—

a husband's mother's neighbor
or some distant relative illusory as smog
blown out to sea. When her turn

at the register comes, the cashier says,
Have a nice day, turning already to the next
in line, grabbing something else to scan.

At the Homeopathic Clinic

Surrounding the squat building
in a dead Pennsylvanian burg,

husks of steel mills rust in autumn jackets,
moaning wind scattering flakes like seeds.

A sign warns, *No food. No drinks. No scents.*
And I am left to ponder the coconut shampoo

I'd used this morning as Dawn disappears
behind a door marked *Patients Only.*

The waiting room swims in new age music,
burbling water and flutterings of a reed flute.

Brochures slotted in an oak rack proclaim
the power of tea, acupuncture, ayurvedic healing.

On a coffee-colored couch, an Indian mother works
a folded newspaper's crossword, foot tapping,

embroidered white flowers dancing on billowy,
black pants. I can't tell if it's she who's sick

or her young son, kneeling on the floor, mesmerized
by a game that looks like a glass pincushion

filled with marbles. One by one, he eases
out the lancing rods, tongue tip jutting

from squeezed lips like a curious mouse.
Suspended, the pent-up marbles are like all

of life’s mysteries, weight of so many wonders
dependent on each other, the slight shifting

of any one threatening to force the rest
into the raucous tumble of a sudden crash.

Little Things That Disappear

I didn't realize they were gone—wistful dreams
once talked about at night, hopes hungered for

like famished wolves—until the fridge
howled lamentations beneath

a fluorescent moon. Empty magnets
clung to its banana-yellow skin

like lonely commuters on a city bus. Absent
were pictures clipped in lustful crazes—

Amazonian zip-lines, palazzos in Rome, sailboats
anchored in the Caribbean's turquoise waters.

One day, we promised, *one day,*
mantra gleaming like pearls

and polished gold, treasure
buried beneath an X,

certain we would never
lose our map.

Things Left Unsaid

What I meant to say this morning
as you divvied pills into a plastic case
with slots for days of the week,

was that sparkles dancing on your cheek—
light refracted from the suncatcher
in the window—reminded me of our trip

to Pennington Gap, that steep drive
up the mountain, nosing through clouds
until we kissed the very blue of heaven.

Those were the days of *Yes,*
when we looked past strangling vines
of kudzu to notice the rock face

of a grandfather speaking from a wall of slate,
his shadowed mouth a cupful of promise.
No wonder we stopped at the glass studio

whose sign advertised "Lessons."
Fearlessly, you plunged your
dye-dipped "gather" into the kiln's

glowing heart, furnace hot enough
to transmute bone to chalk.
When you blew into the spinning rod

and molten glass expanded into
a silver-streaked globe, I could tell
you believed anything was possible.

That is what I meant to say this morning
but didn't, gazing absently at your hands
as each pill plunked into its proper bin.

Dictionary of the Dying

Cancer is not me, Dawn says,
thumping her chest,
that spot where the spot
in her lung

debates every word.
                    Biopsies,
            lymphocytes,
rates of transmission.

How fast the terminally ill
race to new language,
shock of diagnosis
like the bang

of a starter's pistol.
Nothing to do but run
as oncologists
offer lexicon

like Dixie cups
sloshing with water.
                    Cancer
was once too noxious

for my tongue to utter.
Now I chew around the rough.
Like figs. Like chicken bones.
Like crust on day-old pie.

Hurricane

A swirling eye blossoms
in the Atlantic, a white rose
in a field of blue, its whimsical
course swerving and jinking
like a drunk coming home
from the bar.

Dawn refuses to evacuate,
hunkering down after raiding
Food Lion, wheeling out cartfuls
of bottled water and cans
of Chef Boyardee.

She stows patio furniture
then duct-tapes windows
before settling into
her living-room refuge,
focusing on the coming storm,
glad for the tangible fight.

One day's forecasts predict ruin,
the next, good fortune. Back and forth
like all of life's vicissitudes,
never knowing until the last
plucked petal whether
someone loves you,
loves you not.

Road Therapy

Long hair wrapped in a bun
pinned behind her head,

she dons a full-face helmet and gloves,
biker jacket and studded pants.

Sliding into platform boots
she mounts her Honda 450,

a motorcycle three times her weight.
Daily despairs loosen

their bony grip with every mile.
Sheathed in gray leather, rocketing

like an androgynous missile,
cutting wind like the tip

of a plunging spear that knows
nothing but forward motion,

she leans into the road's music—
backbeat of steel-belted rubber,

tree-lined streets chanting
from heartwood at the center

of every ring, echoing pulse
thrumming within her hurtling chest.

Eulogy for the Not-Yet Dead

Crenellated spires of a gothic church
spear the sky, haloed saints weeping
in stained-glass splendor. Scores
of black-clad mourners pack
the cavernous nave's stiff pews—
men in crisp suits, women in dresses
and lace-veiled hats, handkerchiefs
daubing wet eyes as sobs squawk
like swooping magpies.

Resting atop a bier draped
in white linen, a red oak casket
luxuriates in a beam of sun,
your face spotlighted amid its ruffles.
And there I stand beside you like
a conductor without his baton.
I'll never know what words
might spill from my lips
for this is when I always
wake bathed in sweat.

Turning to study your still form,
I wonder if today is *the day.*
Should I hold a mirror
to your mouth to see if fog
will offer resurrection?
Or should I roll over
and close my eyes,
hoping this time to finally
dream of something else?

Mimosa Tree

She loved the way its nyctinastic leaves
shook off dew and opened every morning,
tight fists unclenching to grab the sun,
bundled boughs arching over grass,
exotic fans shading half her yard.

As spring bloomed with wispy crowns—
each spiked with dozens of tiny flowers,
white stems pink at tips like strings
of pulled taffy—she kicked a basketball
for Rottweilers to chase with flashing teeth.

When roots knuckled the driveway
and threatened to buckle
the house's foundation,
radiating across concrete
like ripples on a pond,
she was reminded how often
love is steeped in pain.

Knowing what must be done
but not if she'd have the strength,
she knelt clutching her bow saw
like a rosary, kissing the bark once
before sawing through soft wood
like amputating a gangrenous leg,
leaving behind ghosts of its knee,
its shin, its foot and the way
its toes once wriggled regret
for every suffocating shoe.

Singer

She used to mend my seat-blown pants
as I watched her thread a needle,
press fabric beneath a silver plate,

mesmerized by her deft touch as
spool-pin pistoned and bobbin clacked
like a flamenco dancer's castanets.

Music of chores may compose a symphony.
Mowing the lawn, each turn a dance,
crisp patterns chasing lines of grass

like the formality of a waltz.
Dawn and I used to suddenly burst
into song—cartoon themes, jingles,

or our own invented babble, just because,
just because. Now everything is tiptoe
and hush, tongues too heavy for hymns.

Stuffing my ruined socks in a drawer,
I skirt her sewing machine, touching
its brass Singer nameplate as I pass.

I Never Know When It's Going to Rain

While my eyes spin the carousel of R.E.M.,
Dawn is transfixed by a meteorologist

beside a map of swirling Rorschachs
divining the next day's weather

like tea leaves in the bottom of a cup.
Each night she watches local news,

tiny terrors magnified and given teeth
then tucked beside her as she tries

to fall asleep. In daylight, she shakes
her head at my choice of wardrobe,

the way I dress each day according
to the day before. Cold snaps

and heat waves catch me off guard.
I step into each like a punch-drunk

boxer offering up his chin.
If it rains, I get wet and she laughs.

But most days she studies me
like a kid pressed against

a toy store's display window.
You don't know how lucky you are,

she says beneath her umbrella.
And what can I do but crowd in

beside her as cascading drops
thrum the fabric—a confirmation

of all she knows; for me
the drumbeat of surprise.

Giving Up

Two hours into another drive to Duke,
this time a pre-op visit for radical surgery,

Dawn announces she's giving up. I forget,
for a moment, that we're playing a game,

scanning billboards and bumpers
for letters of the alphabet. My mind

slipping instead into the top drawer
of her vanity where she keeps

a .38 special in a velvet bag.
I remember the game just before

opening my mouth, before stating
I wouldn't stand in her way.

III.
AFTER

Deus Ex Machina

> *Oh, Zeus, you are everywhere, pursuing your noiseless path,*
> *ordering the affairs of mortals according to justice.*
> —Hecuba in *The Trojan Women* by Euripides

Heavy are the hours
beneath night's glassy eye,

the coming surgery
that consumes

all thought, fear
ablaze in our bed

while autumn howls
outside the window.

The surgeon plans
to excavate

Dawn's chest
to remove a wedge

of cancer-spotted lung.
As much chance

of killing as curing,
he'd warned.

What else
is there to say

except goodbye,
just in case,

memorizing her face,
her soft body,

the way her spine
curls against me

as I wrap one
thick arm around

her damaged chest.
She worries what her death

will mean for me,
task of calling others

with the news, each
ripping anew the wound.

Even in a cancer ward
Euripides can astonish,

gods and their miracles
entering from wings.

The doctor who'd explained
the radical procedure

gapes at the latest X-rays,
the white spot predicted

to spread to other organs
now one-third smaller instead.

Everything else is lost
in daze, euphoria,

and the rock
that had been my heart

becomes a sparrow
fluttering within ribs.

A gilded chariot offers
exodus to Mount Olympus,

and what can we do
but run before Zeus

changes his fickle mind?
We fly down the hall,

posters of bald patients
and brave smiles

overlooked in our rush
past reception,

out the door,
stumbling into daylight.

A Galaxy of Astronauts

What should we call them? Dawn asks,
standing before a diorama of colonists on Mars,

part of a NASA exhibit at the art center
nestled in a crook between a turtle-filled lake

and a forest of stately elms. Too long
since we've played this game, inventing

collective nouns like a bristle of goatees,
a corruption of politicians, a gamble of dice,

each phrase threaded through with glee,
the pure thrill of standing shoulder to shoulder

while sectioning our world. In 1486, Juliana Berners
penned terms of venery, every animal herded

into an appropriate stall—a murder of crows,
a blessing of narwhals, a parliament of owls.

And though Dawn's tumor keeps shrinking with every
follow-up to the oncologist, there is one term

from the *Book of Saint Albans* that we skip
like an open manhole cover—*a mutation of thrushes,*

so named from the Medieval belief that the birds
shed their legs every ten years to spawn new ones

in their stead. Leaving the glass case where
tiny men in white spacesuits cluster on red dirt,

we pass replicas of Space Shuttle Atlantis and
the International Space Station, then pause beside

a black-and-white photo of a footprint stamped
in regolith, the rugged outline surviving decades

in atmosphereless powder. Dawn presses her hand
to the glass, and I can tell by her faraway gaze that

she's been transported to the moon. When she blinks
and comes back to Earth with starlight in her eyes,

with all the universe swirling through her lungs,
she carries the answer to her own question.

A Galaxy of Astronauts, she whispers, as if not wanting
to disturb the dust. *That's what we'll call them.*

Death Day

A year ago, the oncologist, eyes downcast,
shoulders slumped, said that *today*

was as far as she might live.   Afterwards,
          time compressed its seasons,

autumn's encroaching loss, winter's stark reality,
a spring not meant to bloom   that somehow did.

What to do when forecasts prove wrong,
when hurricanes meant to batter shore

veer into open water, when expiration date
marked on your carton in bold, block letters

          is struck through, replaced with a blank?

Today, Dawn was supposed to expunge *tomorrow*
from her vocabulary, and I was supposed to begin

my long trek from the first station of grief.
Instead, we go to Busch Gardens, where skinny teens

cast sideways glances at the two old farts in line.
When our turn comes, we board the Big Bad Wolf,

the roller coaster that suspends its passengers,
feet dangling as they hurtle into the future,

jinking this way and that, everyone screaming,
uncertain when the next drop will come.

Burying Morgan

Digging is slow in the gully behind Dawn's house
where willow oaks and gumballs stand sentinel,

stark boughs thatching sky like a crown of thorns.
Ground hard with coming winter, every stab

of the flat-headed shovel is fire in my palms,
root-riven clay refusing to budge, as if

even the earth wants to delay this moment.
Dawn shivers like a baby sparrow

knocked from nest, sleeves of her down jacket
slick with blood. An hour earlier, we'd sprawled

on the veterinarian's floor, Morgan between us
as the bulging tumor in her mouth hemorrhaged,

each of us saying, over and over,
What a good girl,   *what a good girl,*

until the needle plunged and she shuddered
one last time. Now, we cradle her limp body

and feed it to this gaping mouth,
hoping it might swallow our sorrow.

Refilling the hole, I tamp down clumps,
and Dawn plants a daylily, a bulb

whose yellow bloom will crack soil
once the cold of winter has passed.

Stardust

Funny how I forgot what a miracle it is
to be alive at all. Cauldrons of distant stars

compressing heavy elements, supernovas
ejecting them into space, infinitesimal particles

coalescing into planetary matter—each step
essential to fabricate the landscape I now inhabit.

The split-level home, the back deck, the lime-green
Adirondack chair that cups me in its palm.

A trillion deaths created me, creatures spat
by tide onto land, sprouting arms and legs,

mastering fire, surviving long enough to pass along
strands of DNA that spiral in my genes. Coincidence

and happenstance, a fantastic freak of nature,
a myriad millennia of right turns instead of left.

Now, beneath the connect-the-dot of constellations,
the television and all its terrifying news turned off,

stardust beating in my heart and flowing through
veins, I gaze at the moon's half-bit crescent

and ask myself what happens to its other three quarters
when I'm not paying attention.

Alchemy

Between derivations of gravity
and universal laws of motion,
Isaac Newton dabbled in chemistry,
dousing base metals in search

of the Philosopher Stone—
a combination that could raise
gold from rubble, coaxing
a gilt phoenix from ashes.

Experiments continued
even after self-poisonings
and a nervous breakdown.
Scientists of his day

were fascinated by rust,
befuddled by slow spread
of red across iron's surface
like fog across a windowpane.

Alchemy, they called it, transformation
of one substance into another.
Oxidation, we call it today,
its magic demystified,

just as years from now
(decades? centuries?),
when cancer has been cured,
schoolchildren will laugh

at our ignorance, the rube-like way
we gaped at the sequined,
sawn-in-half assistant, certain
she would never again stand whole.

About the Author

The author of five poetry collections, one book of fiction, and hundreds of articles, Bill Glose was named the *Daily Press* Poet Laureate in 2011, was featured by NPR on *The Writer's Almanac* in 2017, and won the Library of Virginia Award for Fiction in 2023. A former editor of *Virginia Adversaria* and much-published writer in multiple genres, he received the F. Scott Fitzgerald Short Story Award and the Dateline Award for Excellence in Journalism. His poems appear in journals, including *The Missouri Review, Rattle, Poet Lore, Narrative Magazine,* and *The Sun.* Bill has taught more than 100 writing classes and workshops at universities, prisons, VA hospitals, conferences, and writers' events. He attends poetry events throughout the state and films the readings, posting over 1,500 of these videos on the YouTube channel Virginia Poetry Online. He's served the Poetry Society of Virginia as President Pro Tempore, Vice President (Eastern Region), Secretary, Poetry Festival Chairman, and judge in numerous contests. His website includes a page of helpful information for writers.

www.BillGlose.com

Virginia Poetry Online:
youtube.com/@virginiapoetryonline5270

www.ingramcontent.com/pod-product-compliance
Lightning Source LLC
LaVergne TN
LVHW090532110826
845146LV00003B/1064

* 9 7 9 8 9 0 1 4 6 8 9 9 9 *